Becoming a Strong Christian

Book Two of the Duncan-Williams Youth Series

Archbishop Nicholas Duncan-Williams

A GOSHEN PUBLISHERS PAPERBACK   VIRGINIA

Becoming a Strong Christian
Book Two

ISBN: 978-0-9994003-8-8
Copyright ©2019 Nicolas Duncan-Williams

Published in 2019
by:

GOSHEN PUBLISHERS LLC
P.O. Box 1562
Stephens City, Virginia, USA
www.GoshenPublishers.com

Our books may be purchased in bulk for promotional, educational, or business use. Please email Agents@GoshenPublishers.com.

First Edition 2019

Cover designed by Goshen Publishers LLC

The Duncan-Williams Youth Series seeks, among several others, to bless you in the following ways:

1. Help you totally yield your life and your future to God, trusting and depending wholly on Him;

2. Equip and challenge you to build and maintain a vibrant intimate relationship with God so you can navigate the journey of life more decisively;

3. Help you become a man or woman of prayer, drawing power from your fellowship with God to deal with situations in your life;

4. Get you to pay closer attention to the value of the family of God on earth, so you can stay with the brethren and not become an easy target of the enemy;

5. Help you identify sin in its forms and resolve to confront sin with the principles and power of God;

6. Dare you to be different in your generation that is heavily influenced by immorality and godlessness, and thereby walk in integrity, honoring God in your life always;

7. Assist you to discover and develop your God-given talents and spiritual gifts by which you can offer acceptable service in the house of God;

8. Help you develop Christian character as the foundation for a future life of leadership and purpose;

9. Challenge you to share your faith in Christ as per the gospel, and God's power unto salvation without fear, and become a good evangelist for God;

10. Help you know how to draw strength from the Holy Spirit, stand in the position of authority, and walk in victory in all the issues confronting you as a growing person; and

11. Help you understand and develop healthful habits in relating with the opposite sex, and thereby prepare for a meaningful marriage and family life.

BECOMING A STRONG CHRISTIAN

Book Two

Other Publications in this series:

- ✓ Book 1: Beginning with God

- ✓ Book 3: Developing Intimacy with God

- ✓ Book 4: Setting Yourself apart unto God

- ✓ Book 5: Discovering and Walking in Purpose

All by Archbishop Nicholas Duncan-Williams

This book belongs to

_____

[Name]

CONTENTS

INTRODUCTION

I trust that after reading my book, *Beginning with God*, you made the most important decision every person should make early in life – to give your life over to the Lord Jesus Christ.

I trust also that you were blessed as you studied the stages of life and identified your current phase.

Having understood the stages you go through and the importance of beginning with God, I want you to understand the processes involved in developing your spiritual life. You need to develop your spiritual life to give you that constant strength you need to go through the rest of your life. This new life is not lived in one's own strength. It is lived in the strength of the Lord and you need to understand how that happens.

God knows very well that in your own strength you cannot do anything right at any time. Remember what Jesus told His disciples: "Without Me ye can do nothing."

> ⁴ *Abide in Me, and I in you. As the branch cannot bear fruit of itself, unless it abides in the vine, neither can you, unless you abide in Me.*
>
> ⁵ *I am the vine, you are the branches. He who abides in Me, and I in him, bears much fruit; for without Me you can do nothing.*
>
> ⁶ *If anyone does not abide in Me, he is cast out as a branch and is withered; and they gather them and throw them into the fire, and they are burned.*
>
> John 15:4-6

That is exactly the picture. The Christian life is actually the life Christ lived. It means only He can live that life. If He has called us to be His children, He expects us to live like Him. That is why He told the disciples to wait in Jerusalem to be endowed with power first, before they attempt anything in His absence. If you have read your Bible very well, you can tell the difference between the disciples before and after their Pentecost experience. God's power available to the believer makes all the difference.

Anyone who tries to live the Christian life in his own strength will fail several times over. The Apostle Paul teaches that it is only in Christ that you can do all things.

In this book, I want to show you the fundamental unchanging practices by which every child of God can access God's power.

1.

GOD IS THE SOURCE OF ALL STRENGTH

The first encounter we have of God as revealed in the Bible is that He is a powerful being. This message is what is made abundantly clear in the creation of the world. In creation God is revealed as the Creator.

> ¹ *In the beginning, God created the heavens and the earth.*
>
> ² *The earth was without form and void, and darkness was over the face of the deep. And the Spirit of God was hovering over the face of the waters.*
>
> ³ *And God said, "Let there be light," and there was light.*
>
> ⁴ *And God saw that the light was good. And God separated the light from the darkness.*
>
> ⁵ *God called the light Day, and the darkness he called Night. And there was evening and there was morning, the first day.*

Genesis 1:1-5

He created by simply speaking. If someone brings new things into being by simply speaking, then you know that it is not mere words the person is speaking. The person is demonstrating power, mighty power.

In a biology class they teach you what living things do and what differentiates living things from non-living things. They teach you that living things breathe, reproduce, move, etc.

What they do not teach you is that for living things to do all that, they need to be alive. The life that living things possess before they can do things is power from God. It is God's power that energizes the cell organelles to perform various functions. The power for cell division, cell multiplication, and cell differentiation that results in the various organs of the human body all receive power from God. Germination of seeds and the transition from seed to flower all draw from God's power.

God's power keeps the planets revolving in their orbits without crashing into each other. The earth and moon will never collide, nor will the earth bump into the sun. The power of God keeps them all in their orbits and we have a harmonious universe!

> *God hath spoken once; twice have I heard this; that power belongeth unto God.*
>
> Psalm 62:11

> *It is he who made the earth by his power, who established the world by his wisdom, and by his understanding stretched out the heavens.*
>
> Jeremiah 10:12

Human history is full of evidence of the power of God.

The life that lies ahead of you is a long journey. It is a journey that requires a lot of preparation. It is not as if there is a point in time when you can say that you have adequately prepared enough for life. In other words, there is no point in time when you can say that you have enough strength to go through the rest of your life. You increase in strength as you go along because the issues you encounter also differ in the strength with which they come attacking you.

King David knew the source of his strength and that led him to write this psalm:

> 5 *My soul, wait thou only upon God; for my expectation is from him.*
>
> 6 *He only is my rock and my salvation: he is my defense; I shall not be moved.*
>
> 7 *In God is my salvation and my glory: the rock of my strength, and my refuge, is in God.*
>
> 8 *Trust in him at all times; ye people, pour out your heart before him: God is a refuge for us. Selah.*

Psalm 62:5-8

When we become God's children by faith in Christ, we have the potential to manifest all of God's characteristics, including His mighty power. If only we can walk in God's power, nothing shall be impossible to us. The problem is that God's power does not automatically come to us because it is our inheritance. God has outlined a process by which we can have His power to deal with all the issues of this life. If you want to experience fulfillment of God's purpose for your life, then you must go through the process by which God's power becomes available.

2.

KNOWING WHAT GOD IS SAYING -
THE BIBLE

When you became born again, you became like a baby in Christ. In fact, the Bible calls the young Christian, irrespective of his age, a newborn babe. The Apostle Peter exhorts us this way:

> ¹ *Wherefore laying aside all malice, and all guile, and hypocrisies, and envies, and all evil speakings,*
>
> ² *As newborn babes, desire the sincere milk of the word, that ye may grow thereby*

> 1 Peter 2:1-2

Jesus said man shall not live by bread alone but by every word that proceeds out of the mouth of God. It means you must know what God has said since the creation of the world.

Now that you have become God's child, your life must be according to what your heavenly Father expects of you. Formerly you were living according to what your heart told you. You did things that you felt were okay, some of which you knew too well that they were not okay, but you went ahead and did them anyway.

Now, this new life demands that you do things differently. But how can you do things differently if you do not know exactly what is expected of you in this new life that has just been introduced to you?

The answer is simple, but it usually does not come out that simple. It is God who said you are a sinner and you need to be saved. It is the same God who told you that you need not do anything for you to be saved because He has made His Son pay for your sins by dying on the cross. It is the same God who said now that you have believed in Jesus Christ as your Savior you have become His child.

What is the logical thing to do if you want to know how to live as a child of God? That has a simple answer, but people often struggle with it. Go back to the same God and find out what He is saying again. You can never go wrong if you go back to God and ask Him what to do to grow in your Christian life.

The only way you can know what God wants you to know is to study His word. God has inspired His servants to write down His word in the Bible. You have to understand that the Bible is the infallible word of God. It comes to us as a history book that is very unique. Its uniqueness lies in the fact that it is the story of God's relationship with the children of Israel, whom He chose to show Himself to the rest of the world.

The Bible was written over a span of 1500 years, by 40 writers. Think of the Bible as the greatest history book ever written. It is a recording of facts, events, places, and people who lived and did things in real time. It is not a novel or mystery, nor something philosophical that causes you to struggle to relate.

Archaeologists, after long years of continual research, are beginning to validate the facts recorded in the Bible. They are affirming the names of the prominent personalities and places including leaders, kings, cities, and events written in the Bible. All these affirm that the Bible is truly historical; it is not a myth or someone's opinion.

God used the writers' own writing styles and personalities to reveal the information about Him that He wants us to know. Knowing about God is the first step to walking with Him.

It is clear that God was behind the scenes and He influenced the thoughts of the writers and, in some cases, told them exactly what to write because some of the things in the Bible cannot be written by man. How will we know the story of creation except God literally tells the writer? God inspired the writing of the Bible. Paul wrote to Timothy to establish this fact:

> [16] *All scripture is given by inspiration of*
> *God, and is profitable for doctrine, for*

reproof, for correction, for instruction in righteousness:

[17] *That the man of God may be perfect, thoroughly furnished unto all good works.*

2 Timothy 3:16-17

In spite of the fact that the people who wrote the Bible lived at different times and it was impossible for some of them to even compare notes, it is clear that they all were addressing one theme – God's redemption story for mankind. That is not surprising because of what I said earlier, that God was behind all the writings.

Listen to what the Apostle Peter said concerning the Bible:

[16] *For we did not follow cleverly devised myths when we made known to you the power and coming of our*

Lord Jesus Christ, but we were eyewitnesses of his majesty.

¹⁷ For when he received honor and glory from God the Father, and the voice was borne to him by the Majestic Glory, "This is my beloved Son, with whom I am well pleased,"

¹⁸ we ourselves heard this very voice borne from heaven, for we were with him on the holy mountain.

¹⁹ And we have the prophetic word more fully confirmed, to which you will do well to pay attention as to a lamp shining in a dark place, until the day dawns and the morning star rises in your hearts,

²⁰ knowing this first of all, that no prophecy of Scripture comes from someone's own interpretation.

²¹ For no prophecy was ever produced by the will of man, but men spoke from God as they were carried along by the Holy Spirit.

2 Peter 1:16-21

Peter is asserting two things here. He is affirming that the Bible is historical. The events happened. He merely attested to what happened at Jesus' baptism, which was a fact of history. He was there in real time, saw everything and heard everything, including the voice they heard from heaven saying that Jesus is God's Son.

The second thing he is teaching here is that there was Someone behind all the writers of the Bible; Someone who was inspiring them to write what they wrote.

If you study the Bible, you can literally trace the story of the fall and redemption of man from the beginning of creation, and through all the years, until God's plan of salvation was openly declared and the Savior of mankind was revealed.

Within this major theme there are other themes. There is one central message consistently carried by all 40 writers of the Bible: God, who created us all, desires a relationship with us. He calls us to know Him and trust Him.

The Bible not only inspires us, but it also explains life and God to us. It does not answer *all* the specific questions we might have; like the exact secondary school or university you should attend, and exactly where you should work after school, the person you should marry, or the specific company you should be working with, but it provides all the principles we should follow in making some of these decisions.

It shows us how to live with purpose and compassion, and how to relate to others. It encourages us to rely on God for strength and direction, and enjoy his love for us. The Bible also tells us how we can have eternal life.

There is a lot of evidence from several sources that support the historical accuracy of the Bible, as well as its claim to divine authorship.

Here are a few reasons you can trust the Bible.

1. The Bible tells us in no uncertain terms where we came from, why we are here, and where we will be going after our lives on earth come to an end.

2. It is the only book that gives explanation to what is happening to us on earth; the deviation from what God initially made us to be. Making us know that we were the ones who broke relationship with God by disobedience, brings knowledge and understanding.

3. It tells us about what God did to reverse the curse we brought upon ourselves and our role in the restoration process.

4. It also alerts us to the nature of the challenges we will face in this journey and how we should conduct our lives so we can always experience victory in whatever comes our way.

5. It address all issues of this life including the following: personal growth and development; personal relationships; marriage and family; career and business; governance; law and order; happiness; sorrow and how to avoid being sorrowful; prosperity and wealth; and how to manage wealth ethically (i.e., what is right and what is wrong) in all endeavors of human life.

6. It is the only text that gives us a glimpse of what lies ahead after we have departed from

here. It is the only book that talks about heaven. The pictures the Bible presents about heaven are very captivating and they strengthen our faith in God's love and faithfulness towards us.

The Bible is not a mere book. It is not like any of the novels you pick from a bookshelf and read. It is a life book. It is the only book that several books have been written from. It is not a book you can forget. It is not a book that you read only on Sundays when you go to church. It is a book of life and living on God's planet earth.

The last thing I want to remind you about the Bible is that it is not a book for Christians only. It is actually God's love letter to all human beings living everywhere on earth. It tells of His love for the people who are living in rebellion against Him and it commissions us to reach out to them.

It is a book for all seasons and all situations. There are people who are following the principles taught in the Bible to do their business, live their marriage and family life, engage in all kinds of ventures, who still may not be Christians. The sad thing about those people is that they are heading into eternity without Christ, unless they are at a point of giving their lives to Christ.

For the Christian, however, the Bible provides the guide map to living in this world as we wait for eternity.

What I have been trying to get you to know is that for the next phase of your life, you need to study God's word, keep it in your heart and let it influence every decision you make.

3.

SPEND TIME WITH GOD'S WORD

Most young growing people today are yet to exercise themselves in sitting down to meditate on God's word. They spend time on their phones, iPads, and all the social media, and have little time allotted to meditating on God's word. Because of this, most young people are not experiencing the blessing that comes from the practice of meditating on God's word.

Let's see God's instruction concerning that. The first one is what God told Joshua after he took over from Moses to lead the children of Israel into the Promised Land. Hear God's word for yourself:

> *This book of the law shall not depart from your mouth, but you shall meditate on it day and night, so that you may be careful to do according to all that is written in it; for then you will make your way prosperous, and then you will have success*
>
> Joshua 1:8

See what the Holy Spirit led the greatest worshipper of all times, King David, to write about God's word in the life of the believer in Christ:

> ¹ *Blessed is the man who walks not in the counsel of the wicked, nor stands in the way of sinners, nor sits in the seat of scoffers;*
>
> ² *but his delight is in the law of the LORD, and on his law he meditates day and night.*
>
> ³ *He is like a tree planted by streams of water that yields its fruit in its season, and its leaf does not wither. In all that he does, he prospers*

> Psalm 1:1-3

Note that what God said directly to Joshua and what the Spirit led David to write have so many things in common. They both result in you becoming prosperous and having good success. The Psalmist says that you will bear your fruit in due season. In other words, everything you desire for your life will come at the right time God has appointed and nothing shall prevent them from coming – good education, good job, good person to marry, and everything good will come in due season if you continue meditating on God's word and living by it.

With the many benefits associated with knowing what God says in His word, many still struggle to keep a consistent habit of spending time to search the Scriptures and asking God for insights into what His word says on every issue of life.

The following will help you enjoy time spent in the word of God and get the most out of it:

Always desire to know that God's mind is on any issue that confronts you . That desire is powerful enough to drive you to make time for God. Jesus said, "Blessed are they which do hunger and thirst after righteousness: for they shall be filled" (Matthew 5:6). Any desire you have toward God is acknowledged by Him and He helps not only to sustain that desire, but the Holy Spirit also helps you discipline yourself to sit at Christ's feet to study His word and meditate on it. You can do it.

Be open to accept what God says on any issue of life. This means you study God's word with an open heart, ready to change your earlier opinions and accept what God is saying. Without this openness you will read God's word and still hold on to your personal opinions. In that case you are in charge, not God.

If you read something from God's word that is in direct conflict with what you have heard people say, you are better off taking what God is revealing to you than hold on to men's opinions. Let God be God.

Set aside specific times of the day when you will come into God's presence only to meditate on portions of His word. This is your devotional hour. I am calling it devotional hour not because you spend one hour for that. For some, early in the morning is best because when the day starts there are many things that compete for their time and before long, their day is gone without hearing from God's word. You can use a good devotional guide. For this purpose, I have developed my devotional, The Lamp. The Lamp captures my thoughts and the lessons God has taught me over the years.

In addition to the devotional hour, establish times when you will take the Bible and do a study of themes, doctrines, and any topic that is of interest to you. This is usually an extended period that may go on for one, two, or even three hours, depending on how you plan your schedule. You can start using concordances and Bible commentaries which help you find what you want and also provide some form of explanation, background information and help you get the best of the study. Note that the time to do a serious study is different from the devotional when you want a theme to occupy you for the rest of the day.

Do well to memorize the Scriptures. Your relationship with the Holy Spirit is greatly enhanced if your heart is full of the word of God. He brings into remembrance the Scriptures piled up in your heart. If there are no Scriptures in your heart, the Holy Spirit has nothing to work with. As a young person with tremendous memory power, you can memorize a Scripture everyday if you decide.

You get the best when you do both a devotional hour [Quiet Time] as well as a time of prolonged Bible study. Don't let one of them suffer.

The word of God comes alive when you practice what you learn in the designated periods. That takes you from being only a hearer of the word to a doer of the word. It is in doing what the word says that the word sticks with you.

> [9] *How can a young man keep his way pure? By guarding it according to your word.*

¹⁰ *With my whole heart I seek you; let me not wander from your commandments!*

¹¹ *I have stored up your word in my heart, that I might not sin against you.*

¹² *Blessed are you, O LORD; teach me your statutes!*

¹³ *With my lips I declare all the rules of your mouth.*

¹⁴ *In the way of your testimonies I delight as much as in all riches.*

¹⁵ *I will meditate on your precepts and fix my eyes on your ways.*

¹⁶ *I will delight in your statutes; I will not forget your word.*

Psalm 119:9-16

Tell yourself you are going to be an exceptional young person, by making God's word abide bountifully in your heart to guide you in all your endeavors. That is a sure foundation with which to confront the challenges life throws at you during the adult years.

Concerning the word, Moses wrote to the children of Israel,

> 8 *You shall bind them as a sign on your hand, and they shall be as frontlets between your eyes.*
>
> 9 *You shall write them on the doorposts of your house and on your gates.*
>
> Deuteronomy 6:8-9

The above passage literally means everywhere you are, the word of God is with you one way or the other. Keep it on cards. Let it be on your electronic media, on your exercise machines, and notebooks; practically everywhere that you can see just by a simple glance.

Compose short music with it, rap it, tell it to your friends, just make sure in all you do, God's word comes alive.

My plan for spending time with God's word:

_____

_____

_____

_____

_____

_____

_____

4.

SPEND TIME TALKING WITH GOD

Can you imagine that you wake up in the morning and say nothing to your dad? You just draw lines around him in the house until you are ready to go out and then you go to him and ask for money? What do you expect to happen?

If for the whole period you are on vacation you spend the time on your phone chatting with your friends and have no time to talk with your dad about school, your performance, and what you need for school; and then all of a sudden, you present him with a bill one week to reopening for him to provide money for your education. You can immediately tell what the atmosphere would feel like. That is what may happen if you treat your heavenly Father like that.

What most people don't understand is that prayer is not an activity we engage to get God's attention to do what we want him to do for us.

Prayer is born out of the understanding that you now have a heavenly Father who loves you and, therefore, you also desire to speak with Him all the time.

With that understanding you do not go to God only when you need him to give you something or do something for you. That is not the essence of prayer. The essence of prayer is fellowship with heavenly Father who loves to hear you and also speak with you.

Prayer is the breath of your spiritual life. If you don't pray it is like you are suffocating to die. Actually, when you don't pray, you end up dying spiritually because you cut off the link between you and the Source of life – your heavenly Father.

A strong prayer life is born out of the understanding that without God you cannot do anything. You have to get to the point where you accept that you cannot move the next step of your life without God.

Jesus sets the example for us to follow:

35 And rising very early in the morning, while it was still dark, he departed and went out to a desolate place, and there he prayed.

36 And Simon and those who were with him searched for him,

37 and they found him and said to him, "Everyone is looking for you."

38 And he said to them, "Let us go on to the next towns, that I may preach there also, for that is why I came out."

39 And he went throughout all Galilee, preaching in their synagogues and casting out demons.

Mark 1:35-39

Note the following about Jesus' example:

1. He rose up early in the morning. That most probably means before everyone else woke up. The only reason He would do that was to

have private time with the heavenly Father. That makes the morning a very appropriate time to spend before God. Jesus withdrew from them all to avoid being interrupted.

You have to understand that time reserved for God is His time. Nothing whatsoever should compete with that time. Power your phone off and keep it away from you to completely eliminate the interruption.

Note that if Jesus had not hidden Himself from everyone else, He would have been interrupted by so many people who wanted to speak with Him. Listen to what the disciples said to Him, "Everyone is looking for you." By "everyone," they could mean the 12 disciples; or they could mean the crowds waiting to hear from Him or see Him perform miracles. Believe me, you will always have someone wanting to talk to you at any time; so, you have to intentionally block them out so you can be with Jesus.

Jesus made a very important statement here. He said they could now go out and preach and that was why He had come out of the hiding place. Being in the hiding place with the Father alone provided the freshness of power He needed to preach and perform the miracles He did. You may not necessarily be out there performing miracles exactly like Jesus did, but for whatever you do in your life, you are guaranteed one thing; that the more time you spend with the Father in private, the more His grace and power rubs over you to do whatever you do.

That is when your friends will begin to see improvement in your academics. That is where they see you as different. You are different because you are not yielding to the common temptations everyone is vulnerable to, including you. You are able to walk in extra power because you know how to spend time with your heavenly Father in private.

Practice running away from everyone else and spending time with God and see what a transformation that will come into your life. This is yours for the taking.

> *Take time to be holy, speak oft with thy*
> *Lord;*
> *Abide in Him always, and feed on His*
> *Word.*
> *Make friends of God's children, help*
> *those who are weak,*
> *Forgetting in nothing His blessing to*
> *seek.*

William D. Longstaff, Songwriter

This is just one verse of a hymn that was popular some time ago. These days, we do not often sing those songs.

The youth of today in particular are bombarded with a lot of information on social media. Their attention is captured 24/7 with anything that is readable. It is becoming a challenge for young people to switch off their phones and do anything else.

Remember that time on the phone does not constitute life. It takes you away from life. The fun you have on the phone does not translate into life. It is only the chat you have with your heavenly Father that translates into life for you.

The other challenge is that life in the 21st century is too fast. People have stopped taking time to pause. Before you finish thinking about one thing, you are bombarded with another, each of them demanding your maximum attention. If you ask where the rush is taking you, it is difficult to get a tangible, meaningful answer; yet, people are on the run from one thing to the other. It takes an intentional decision coupled with discipline for today's young people to spend time with God.

I trust that you will plan your life such that time to talk with God will be priority number one!

My plan for spending time
talking with God:

_____

_____

_____

_____

_____

_____

_____

5.

BENEFITS OF PRAYING

In this section, I will focus on some of the benefits that come to people who live a lifestyle of prayer. I call it a lifestyle of prayer because it is not something you do for a week and forget. Most people have a lot of time for other things and not for prayer. I don't want you to miss any of the blessings God gave me because of my commitment to prayer, and that is why I am sharing these few thoughts here. Enjoy reading and make them a part of your Christian experience.

1. Prayer further strengthens your relationship with God.

Anyone who understands relationships knows that there is no mystery about developing a relationship. Relationships grow in proportion to the frequency of interaction you have with the other person. If you have a dog at home and every morning you spend ten minutes playing with that dog before you go out to work, you are unconsciously building a relationship with that dog. Over a period of time, you will begin feeling lonely if you went out without playing with that dog. You could be in the office and be thinking about that dog. You will find yourself reflecting on the last time you played with the dog and what you said to the dog even though you know it is an animal.

Is it different from building a strong relationship with God? I don't think so.

The frequency of your prayer time with God determines how strong or how weak a relationship you have with Him.

People who consistently spend time with God in prayer, are actually building their relationship with God. It is about consistency. This means that if it is 30 minutes you pray every day as of now, and you are consistent with that, you are still growing the relationship. Before you realize it, 30 minutes turns into an hour and the next moment you are spending several hours with God.

If your prayer life becomes consistent, the effect is that you become more conscious of God everywhere you are and in everything you do. You always know that you are God's child and that He is with you wherever you go. That consciousness fills your heart and your entire being. You no longer have doubts as to whether you are a child of God or not. You simply know it!

Can you imagine what goes on in the heart of the child of the president of your country wherever she goes? She is confident; she is conscious that everyone acknowledges that she is the president's daughter. The way she talks and carries herself tells everyone who she is. How about the knowing that you are a child of the living God? You cannot compare anything with that feeling. Guess what? It does not come automatically. Even if the son or daughter of the president does have a good relationship with their father, they are not bold enough to walk into town feeling they are children of the president.

You cannot ignore a deep fellowship with God and still expect to enjoy the feeling that you are God's child anywhere you go.

Prayer gives you direct access to the power of God.

Think of a fountain from which water is flowing in great abundance. If people need water, they simply go to the source, make available their containers, and collect as much water as they need for their daily requirements. Those who come regularly to fetch water are the ones who will always have water in their homes. Those who do not come so frequently will have water in proportion to the frequency at which they come to catch the water that is flowing without stopping.

It is the same with God. He is the source of everything good we expect. How can you have access to all of it when you are constantly moving away from Him?

Jesus knew this principle and He never violated it. He went through due process. Jesus knew how to access power to walk in power. This is what happened before He started His earthly ministry:

> ¹² And Jesus answered him, "It is said, 'You shall not put the Lord your God to the test.'"
>
> ¹³ And when the devil had ended every temptation, he departed from him until an opportune time
>
> ¹⁴ And Jesus returned in the power of the Spirit to Galilee, and a report about him went out through all the surrounding country.
>
> ¹⁵ And he taught in their synagogues, being glorified by all.
>
> Luke 4:12-15

This passage is about the temptation of Jesus. Immediately after His baptism by John in the

Jordan River, Jesus was led by the Spirit into the wilderness. Forty days and nights in the presence of God was God's way to endow Jesus with power. Note the outcome of that endowment. Jesus returned in the power of the Holy Spirit and report went around the whole region concerning Him.

While He lived on earth as a man, Jesus went through all the processes God had ordained by which He works with me amongst men. One of the processes is spending time in prayer with God. Jesus knew that and thereby subjected Himself to the process. If Jesus waited on the Father in prayer to be endowed with power that was testified when He came out, what makes any one of us think that we can dodge from God's presence and still walk in the power of the Holy Spirit?

Now you can understand why He told His disciples to wait in Jerusalem for the promise of the Father. He told them the Holy Spirit would come upon them and then they shall receive power in the process. With that power they shall be His witnesses everywhere in their world.

Remember that the Holy Spirit was poured upon them in the act of prayer. It was when they were in God's presence that the outpouring happened. I am sure they did not know the exact day the Spirit would be poured upon them. They also did not know in what manner it would happen. They simply continued in prayer as Jesus had instructed them. Their obedience brought them great results.

Can you imagine what would happen to you if you make time every weekend to pray in God's presence? After some time, you would walk on campus full of power. You would receive the boldness to share Jesus with your classmates and anyone on campus that comes your way. You would be praying for people who need God's intervention in their lives, and you would see results. You would be amazed looking at yourself, but that is how it happens.

More prayer in God's presence means more power of God for the believer, and this is not restricted to age. It is not meant for the elderly. It is meant for the youth as well.

Listen to what Isaiah the prophet wrote under the unction of the Holy Spirit:

> [28] *Have you not known? Have you not heard? The LORD is the everlasting God, the Creator of the ends of the earth. He does not faint or grow weary; his understanding is unsearchable.*
>
> [29] *He gives power to the faint, and to him who has no might he increases strength.*
>
> [30] *Even youths shall faint and be weary, and young men shall fall exhausted;*
>
> [31] *but they who wait for the LORD shall renew their strength; they shall mount*

up with wings like eagles; they shall run and not be weary; they shall walk and not faint.

Isaiah 40:28-31

God gives power to the faint irrespective of their age. If you feel weak and faint, go wait upon the Lord and get yourself some power to confront the issues of your life. They will bow to the power that God endows in you. It is a way that will not change because God is faithful. God uses the eagle to illustrate what happens to those who spend time with Him. The eagle is perceived as a strong bird that can fly several heights, probably more than any bird can. It is presented as a strong bird. God says you will mount up with wings like the eagle. It is a promise of unlimited power to do exploits beyond your imagination.

Through prayer you receive God's wisdom for our daily living.

We live in a world full of troubles and problems. The interesting fact is that these are troubles we bring upon ourselves. Think of many young people today who would not listen to their parents because they think they have come of age. It is not long before they face the realities of life that have no respect for age.

Fire is fire for anyone of any age. When the crawling child touches fire, the fire would not say that because it is a crawling child it will not burn his fingers. His fingers will surely receive the full impact of fire. Fire burns!

This illustration explains how we end up creating problems for ourselves. The truth about problems is that we have to solve them. Many people have done a lot of trial and error to fix the problems humanity has brought upon itself.

I am sure as a growing person you have also tried your hands at solving some of the problems you created by some decisions you made. By now you know that problems do not go away by wishing them away. They stare us in the face morning, noon, and night.

People go to school to learn; and it is good to learn. I encourage you to go beyond a bachelor's degree, do a master's degree, and even go for your doctorate once you have what it takes to go that far in formal education.

It is essential, however, and you must know the difference between the degrees that men give and the wisdom that God Himself gives. God's wisdom is way above what any university degree can give you, except that university operates in the wisdom of God.

The apostle James gives us this exhortation:

> [5] *If any of you lacks wisdom, let him ask God, who gives generously to all without reproach, and it will be given him.*

> ⁶ But let him ask in faith, with no doubting, for the one who doubts is like a wave of the sea that is driven and tossed by the wind.
>
> ⁷ For that person must not suppose that he will receive anything from the Lord;
>
> ⁸ he is a double-minded man, unstable in all his ways.
>
> *James 1:5-8*

When the Bible says if anyone lacks wisdom it means anyone irrespective of age, social standing, educational attainment, etc. If the man with a PhD degree needs wisdom, let him ask God. The wisdom of God is the only wisdom that can fix the problems we have created for ourselves in this world. Without the wisdom of God, men do a lot of trial and error at solving the world's problems.

If by any means one of their ways works, it is recorded and engrained in metal only to learn at a later date, that the wisdom that solved one problem yesterday is unable to solve a problem today that looks in every way like the one yesterday.

The wisdom of this world is foolishness before God.

> [18] *Let no one deceive himself. If anyone among you thinks that he is wise in this age, let him become a fool that he may become wise.*
>
> [19] *For the wisdom of this world is folly with God. For it is written, "He catches the wise in their craftiness,"*
>
> [20] *and again, "The Lord knows the thoughts of the wise, that they are futile."*
>
> 1 Corinthians 3:18-20

Anyone who operates the wisdom of this world may be seen by the world as wise, but the Bible says it is foolish. What wisdom is there for example in hoarding goods to create scarcity so you can sell it at prices no man can afford? In the eyes of the world, that is economics and people who practice it are deemed to be wise. Before God this is foolishness; it is exploiting the underprivileged.

The other truth about wisdom is that it is not one size fits all. Solomon used wisdom to solve a problem between two women fighting over a child. Today we must use a different method to solve similar problems and we need wisdom for today!

Jesus described Himself as greater than Solomon. When He was alive people could go to Him and seek wisdom like Nicodemus did. Now that Jesus is no longer physically living in our midst, the only way to get wisdom directly from Him is to go to Him in prayer. If you don't want to walk in this world foolishly, get into your prayer closet and ask God for wisdom like Solomon did. God is still in the business of making people wise. It is yours for the taking. Go for it!

Prayer gives you confidence to face your world.

I am sure you have had the experience of going out there when you were a kid, and someone tried bullying you and you came home to tell your big brother. Your big brother told you if someone tried it again, tell them that your big brother will sort him out. Your big brother came around once and people saw him and realized he meant business with what he said. From that time onward, you did not walk in school feeling timid and afraid that someone would come bullying. Your big brother may not follow you to school every day, but the thought that He was around was enough to build confidence in you. You walked chest out and told yourself, "no one can mess with me."

One day someone will also bring his big brother who is more macho than your big brother and that will be the end of your confidence.

Now, God is way bigger than your big brother. There is no basis for comparison when it gets to that. God is much greater than anyone else out there who threatens to finish you. There is no one anyone is bringing that is bigger than God.

When you spend time with God on a consistent basis, He pours Himself into you the more. He also speaks His words of assurance to you.

What does God's statement that you are the apple of His eye do to you when you walk around? How about when the devil comes against you like a flood, the spirit of God will raise a standard against him? What about no weapon formed against you shall prosper?

It is obvious that you walk through life chest out, not proud and looking down upon everyone around, but you go through life with a certain level of confidence that nothing you see moves you. It all has got to do with the fact that God is with you everywhere you go. The God in whose presence you spent a good amount of time in the morning does not leave you in the afternoon when you need Him.

All your fears go away and you know that whether it is examinations, or participation in something, God is with you because you just came out of deep fellowship with Him.

Prayer makes you strong to stand against the attacks of the enemy. One of the truths that will hit you early in your Christian life is that life is a battle. In our local parlance we say, "Life is war." We are at war with the devil.

The moment you became born again, you became public enemy number one to the camp of the devil. He will do everything possible to make you not enjoy being a Christian. He cannot kill you, but will do everything such that if possible, make you give up your faith in God.

The Apostle Paul taught explicitly on this when he wrote the following message to the church in Ephesus:

> ¹⁰ *Finally, be strong in the Lord and in the strength of his might.*

¹¹ Put on the whole armor of God, that you may be able to stand against the schemes of the devil.

¹² For we do not wrestle against flesh and blood, but against the rulers, against the authorities, against the cosmic powers over this present darkness, against the spiritual forces of evil in the heavenly places.

¹³ Therefore take up the whole armor of God, that you may be able to withstand in the evil day, and having done all, to stand firm.

Ephesians 6:10-13

Standing in prayer is one of the ways you can thwart the enemy's missiles thrown at you from every direction. The more you stand in prayer the more you experience the victory that Jesus won on the cross for all humanity. Remember Daniel prayed and asked God for something. The Bible says his answer was released the day he started praying. It had to take 21 days of continued prayer because the enemy sent a demon to try to block the answer. Get this account from Daniel:

> [12] *Then he said to me, "Fear not, Daniel, for from the first day that you set your heart to understand and humbled yourself before your God, your words have been heard, and I have come because of your words.*
>
> [13] *The prince of the kingdom of Persia withstood me twenty-one days, but Michael, one of the chief princes, came to help me, for I was left there with the kings of Persia,*
>
> [14] *and came to make you understand what is to happen to your people in the latter days. For the vision is for days yet to come."*
>
> Daniel 10:12-14

Daniel's experience is a classic example and it tells us that we should never give up in prayer when the answer seems to not be coming forth. Your continued prayer will destroy the work of principalities and powers in the heavenly realms that are standing against your progress. When you pray, you win life's battles with the victory of Christ on Calvary.

The Christian who does not go on his knees cannot stand tall in the time of spiritual warfare. It is the kneeling child of God who can stand firm in the face of the greatest conflict.

People of prayer are people of power and the enemy knows that.

Prayer takes us into the throne of Grace.

The writer of Hebrews unveils the truth about prayer and the grace of God for the believer. This is what he says:

Let us therefore come forward with boldness to the throne of grace that we may receive mercy and find grace for timely help.

Hebrews 4:16

Standing before the throne of grace is a wonderful experience you never want to miss. Grace opens the whole counsel of God unto us. There we have access to the unfailing, unending, unchanging love of God. It is this that makes all things available to us. From the throne of grace God gives over and above what we think of or ask. This is what Jesus said about asking from God.

> [23] *In that day you will ask nothing of me. Truly, truly, I say to you, whatever you ask of the Father in my name, he will give it to you.*
>
> [24] *Until now you have asked nothing in my name. Ask, and you will receive, that your joy may be full.*

John 16:23-24

These were some of Jesus' last words to His disciples before He went to the cross. Up to the time He was with them they were not asking anything from the Father because Jesus was still with them. Jesus, therefore, made them understand the changes that would come in the processes of receiving from God. It is simple. They will ask the Father anything in Jesus' name and the Father will grant it unto them.

God knows our needs, and He wants us to ask Him to complete the process. Prayer takes us to the throne of grace where we can ask anything according to what God has planned for us.

There are a few things you must know about the grace of God. Very often we only think of God's grace when we have sinned and need forgiveness. That is only one side of grace.

The other aspect of grace is that it gives us favor before men. When God gives you favor, even your enemies find themselves doing things that bring you the success that you desire. God is able to make your enemies bow to His will for your life.

Grace also has a strong enabling component. The grace of God empowers you to do more than you would have done in your power. Grace is an enabler for the child of God. You are better off drawing from the throne of God because it is a complete package.

My plan for attaining
God's grace:

_____

_____

_____

_____

_____

_____

_____

6.

FELLOWSHIP WITH THE BRETHREN

Let me start this section with a very important verse that I think sometimes believers overlook:

> 23 *Let us hold fast the confession of our hope without wavering, for he who promised is faithful.*
>
> 24 *And let us consider how to stir up one another to love and good works,*
>
> 25 *not neglecting to meet together, as is the habit of some, but encouraging one another, and all the more as you see the Day drawing near.*
>
> Hebrews 10:23-25

When you become born again, you automatically become a member of God's family. God's family is universal in that it is all over the world. It means when you go to China or the United States or Japan or Australia, and you meet Christians there, you are a member of that family. You are welcomed to attend their gatherings and you will receive the welcome that is available to members of the family.

It is just like your family with your siblings. You don't struggle to belong. You just belong and you are welcome by all. Even if you have not seen your brother for weeks or months, when you come to the family meeting called by your dad, you just flow and fit in because you are home. It is the same with belonging to God's family.

Belonging to God's family is even stronger because this is a family you chose to belong to. You did not choose to belong to your biological family. You were planted there by physical birth over which you had no control. With God's family, you made a decision to belong to Jesus. You made a choice. You did it intentionally. Remember that when the trumpet sounds at the rapture, your blood family members who do not have Jesus in their hearts will be left behind. They will be separated from you forever. It is your Christian brethren who will be taken together with you to live with the Lord forever.

That is why the writer of Hebrews exhorts that we make efforts to join and participate in the gatherings of the body of Christ. Note that the writer warns against absenting yourself from the gathering. It means you do not decide to be absent when the family gathers. You make it a choice to be there.

You cannot choose Sunday mornings for doing group assignments in school or plan an excursion on a Sunday morning, because that is typically the time when the church gathers. There may be other meetings organized by the church meant to bring the believers together, and you do not have to miss those.

It amazes me to hear that some people fix business meetings on Sunday when they are supposed to be in church. Remember that God did not give you that business opportunity to take you away from the gathering of the family.

If you find yourself doing that, you are just creating the situation for you to be isolated from the family of God. While in school, don't skip fellowship gatherings for any other thing. Plan to fully participate in the Christian gatherings and get the full blessings.

The benefits of fellowshipping with the saints are numerous. Here are just a few of them:

Continual fellowship with the brethren gives you a sense of belonging. Most people, when they come to Christ, have trouble with their blood families who may not be Christians or belong to another religious group that is antagonistic to the Christian faith. In situations like that the Christian fellowship provides a place of refuge and rest. It provides a home for people who convert from other faiths that reject them because of their faith in Christ.

When we come together, we help each other in various ways. When one member suffers it becomes the responsibility of other members of the family to stand with that person. No one lives on an island in the body of Christ. There is always someone reaching out to you in time of difficulty.

Being active with the family of God also provides opportunity to develop your spiritual gifts and prepare yourself for effective Christian service. Whether you have the gift of singing, to exhort, or even to teach, the family of God provides opportunity to express and develop this gift.

If you remove yourself from the fellowship of believers, you will find yourself in the company of people who do not believe, and that becomes the beginning of the end of your Christian walk. Non-believing fellowships will kill your faith and commitment to God.

It is one of the devil's tricks to gradually get you into backsliding from the Christian faith. As believers in the family, we sometimes have unpleasant experiences with fellow believers, but that is never a license to abandon the family of God and make friends with the people of the world. The price you pay for that is way too high.

My commitment to fellowship with the Brethren:

_____

_____

_____

_____

_____

_____

CONCLUSION

It takes strong Christians serving God selflessly to make the kingdoms of this world become the kingdoms of our God and King. You have a critical part to play so do not live as a weak Christian. Grow to be strong and play your part to make God's plan come to pass. You will certainly be blessed and highly rewarded by God.

www.ingramcontent.com/pod-product-compliance
Lightning Source LLC
Chambersburg PA
CBHW071817020426
42331CB00007B/1521